grist

Anna Elliston

BookLeaf Publishing

India | USA | UK

Presentation by *BookLeaf Publishing*

Web: www.bookleafpub.com

E-mail: info@bookleafpub.com

ISBN: 978-93-5744-982-3

First edition 2022

Dedication

To Nysha, gem-friend

to Shauna, light-filled being

and to my girls

with love and affection

Acknowledgement

Thanks to Bob Elliston and Caroline van Riet and very special thanks, as always, to Jay Wheeler.

Preface

I wrote this collection of poems in
minuscule snatches of time over the
course of October, 2021.

There is dark matter about poetry: the
words not chosen, the space around
and beyond the words on the page, the
things deliberately unsaid. To honour
this, you'll see I've stayed mostly in the
realm of the short-form in these
distillations on parenthood, ecological
breakdown, grief, psychology, bravery,
self-esteem, hope, joy and friendship.

You'll find some of the poems to be very
short indeed. I initially wrote them to be
short enough to fit into a matchbox. I
imagined the reader could carry it in
their pocket and pull it out at the right
moment. I was taken by the idea that a
poem might be carried, not as a worry
or an albatross, but as a gift or a charm.

It has been so enjoyable to delve into writing poetry - what a crystal lens with which to see the world. Maybe I'll return to it some other time.

For now, I hope you enjoy and thank you for reading.

If you are interested in more of my writing, you can follow me on Instagram: @anna_e_writes.

All royalties from the sale of this book will go to the Australian Conservation Foundation.

to my past self

you needn't have worried
all was for the good
and if not for the good
it was
for the strengthening
and if not for that
then it was
and it is
deliciously
grist

mess

give global leadership
to parents who feed babies
and in the silence
of the hours before dawn
in that strange grey moonscape
between sleep and wake
we will think a way out
of this mess we're in

it takes

oh mother i see you carry too much
it is a pity
they made you the village
when maybe you needed
to rest awhile
your tender body
sweet tired woman
hush

fathers

most of all, do not absorb
that you are useless. lies.
your love is ballast
without which
we topple:
your children, your daughters
empty hulls
will drift and elsewhere seek a love
that steadies us as yours might have.
do you not see
this pattern woven
into the cloth
of all our sails?

untold

what more caustic an acid
is there
than a story untold
eating us from the inside in
?

soft truth

do you too see
the ghost twin
of vulnerability
is
bravery?
she is behind every act
in which there is a risk
of revealing the soft truth
of ourselves.

on time

do not rob yourself of time
a crime for which
you would be both
villain and victim

vast

the world -
so vast and large
my hands -
so small.
how will i
reconcile this
at all?

delight

a tiny, dimpled fist rests on my chest
and steady breaths whisper to and fro
from the rosebud caramel mouth
of my suckling babe.
i breathe in her sweet milk ferment
and my lips trace
her edible silken skin.
i drift as she dreams.

i think
if i could speak into the ear
of my past self
and tell her
grinningly
how things turn out
delight would spill hot and soak
down to her very bones.

within

i tell myself
(and feel free to join in)
it's no match
for the fire and fury
within

the last pie

world leaders
must just think

one day
when the sea is black and boiling
and the polar bears that floated
away on waning ice floes
are licking meat
from their own sticky bones

on that day
we'll carve up antarctica
like the world's
last
pie,
russia
china
you
and i.

she is not lost

another woman dead,
i think, as i put on
my coat. i wrap myself against it.
her family, her friends –
the horror, oh horror!

i try not to go there in my head
for fear my heart will
shatter red across the floor
and in doing so
i will lose another piece of it
just as she is
not lost –
that implies a blamelessness –
but
obliterated.

[how must i raise
daughters
in this world?]

in spite of us

i have in my head
a supermarket in ruins
two hundred years
into the future.

neon signs hang glowless
vines grow through the freezer section
small mammals nest
in rusting shelves
floor tiles crack with the roots
of trees breaking through
there is wet earth about the air and
the beeping of barcodes
has faded to birdsong.

it softens and slows me
and helps me to think
the earth
will be okay
in spite of us.

bruny island district school
thirty-year reunion

island is calling you

day is wrenblue & faultless
wobbly air climbs from hot bonnets
the ferry queue creeps

sea breeze nicks up whites across the
channel

time thickens
          people wait, hands pocketed &
leaning

somewhere, black cockatoos shriek
          welcome or warning

island is written in you

because elsewhere, you know
sun is crackling on black snakeskin

as the beast moves broodily through dry
grass
more scared of you than you are of it

you hold this wisdom
          like eggs

island has given you
          gutdeep knowings

of bracken thicket & native orchid
spray of dust on potholed roads
roar of surf on unpeopled beaches
feathering of wind through viminalis

still nights smeared with brazen stars

island has rendered you

bare & earth-hearted
strange tangle of music, words & dry
sclerophyll
& always slightly shaken by cities

island receives you

curves of the road like an old song
you forgot you never forgot
ghosts & stories seep, you perspire them

it is more than salt air
pulling you to
          the homeness you seek.

wild

who of us does not ache
to be wild?
who can say they do not dream
to run
through the moonsilk night
cool earth underfoot
to catch the sun rise
between mountains?

shauna's trip

the first time round
all nerves
dizzy like champagne
she found herself
silent
still
in the presence
of a beautiful, light-filled being.
and then – how dazzling, divine!
as a lake reflecting evening
she realised
that being
was herself.

brave

let us talk of the ways in which
bravery is feminine

not just taking bullets
the crunch of boots on gravel
the jutting of the jaw

rather
bravery is raising a rose to the stone
keeping the flesh soft
the heart raw

rise with me

in my ageing
i will not fade
will not lie quiet
as i have subsumed
as rot is to mushroom
that women must
but rather
i will rise
like a golden queen
so i say to you
sister rise with me
we were
born of
and meant for
the stars

gem-friend

After R.D Laing

i feel you holding me &
it is this
that allows me
to hold myself
to cradle sweetly
my bare, wet heart
as i cradle you & yours
that is its
beauty
that is your
power

bold &

future is possible
is precious,
is wondrous, luscious, dear

all you must do,
precious, is -
bold & brave - live your way here

i have

a bird in my hand
a half-full glass
two right sides to my bed

a line in the sand
the greenest grass
and a laurel on which
to rest my head.